The Magic Box

I dedicate this book to my children with love,
Renay, Andrea, Eric and Peter.

The Magic Box

The Eccentric Genius
of
Hannah Maynard

Claire Weissman Wilks

Exile Editions Ltd.
Toronto

Copyright© 1980 by Claire Weissman Wilks.

First published in Canada by
Exile Editions Limited
20 Dale Avenue, Toronto M4W 1K4

Design Assistance by Harold Kurschenska.

Typography by A-Z Graphics Ltd., Toronto.

Published with assistance from The Canada Council, The Ontario Arts Council, and Heritage Trust of British Columbia.

Printed in Canada by Herzig Somerville Limited, Toronto.

ISBN 0-920428-34-7

Introduction

One day, while sifting through prints and glass plates in the Provincial Archives in Victoria, British Columbia, I came across a half-dozen photographs unlike anything I had ever seen. They were taken by a woman, Hannah Maynard, who was known locally by some specialists, but whose work attracted no particular interest. In the archive, I found there were boxes of glass negatives and prints on cardboard mounts — old images unseen in decades. As I held these to the light, it became clear that Hannah Maynard was a woman and a photographer of extraordinary eccentricity and character.

She was born Hannah Hatherly in 1834, in Cornwall. When she was eighteen, she met Richard Maynard, a twenty-year-old apprentice bootmaker who wanted to be a seaman. He worked the coasting trade in the summer, making boots in the winter. They married in 1852 and sailed to Canada. Their first son, George, conceived at sea, was born in the same year in the Canada West town of Bowmanville. Richard set up shop, fathered three more children, and left to follow the 1858 goldrush in the colony of British Columbia. He took a schooner from Boston down the east coast, crossed the Panama isthmus, and sailed up the west coast on the windship *Forward* to Victoria. He prospected for gold on the Fraser River and made considerable money during that season on Hudson Bar. He went home to fetch his wife and found her studying professional photography, probably with R & H O'Hara of Bowmanville, Photographers, Booksellers, Insurance Agents, Etc.

Richard sold the boot store and they set sail for Victoria. They arrived on the decrepit *Sierra Nevada* from San Francisco and Hannah found that Victoria, in 1862, was a small outpost town boasting thirty-seven brick buildings, but makeshift around the edges, a city, Hannah said, "of tents, gullies and swamps and the inhabitants mostly miners." There were dandies, too, and thugs, Navy officers and sailors from the tall ships, Blacks and Chinese, and ladies of the saloons and sporting houses. Richard went up the Stikine river, placer mining, and she settled into a board-and-batten house on the outskirts of town, on the dirt track called Johnson Street. It's believed that she opened Mrs. R. Maynard's Photographic Gallery in that year.

In 1863, Richard came home and found her successfully entrenched in her own affairs. Photography, as a profession for a west coast woman, was somewhat unusual, but not as strange as she later liked to make out. She apparently told several people that she had suffered in the shadow of Richard's name, and this story is reflected in a later report in *The Colonist:* "Everyone was astonished. And, like many women who start anything new she was for a long time boycotted by the public...until Victoria got used to a woman photographer, Mr. Maynard frequently pretended that he had taken the pictures, whereas in actual fact it was his wife who had done the job." There is, in fact, no evidence that Richard pretended any such thing. He learned photography at her hand and then took his own pictures. It is possible that she deliberately created the confusion herself by often publishing his landscapes under her name. Whatever the case, Richard opened a boot store and pursued his own photographic interests, confining himself to outdoor work and taking every opportunity to go into the wilderness. Sometimes, however, Hannah went with him and once she went to the Queen Charlotte Islands alone. The result is, many landscape photographs are hers, and a blurring between their work is sometimes unavoidable, but only in the wilderness, for he seldom, if ever, worked in the studio and seems never to have been interested in the experimental possibilities of the camera. He was a diligent man doing his job, and he liked doing it best along the up-country trails, sometimes with his young son.

In 1868, he and Albert, who was eleven years old, went by wagon to the mining town of Barkerville, taking pictures along the Cariboo Road. It was sprawling, wild country. There was brawling and drunkenness in the little depots. Albert, called The General, was, according to a newspaper report, something of a child entertainer: "No more interesting characters ever went to the Cariboo. The General is a man of many sides; in fact, he could take a turn in legerdemain or an acrobatic stunt and the miners were not without entertainment as long as the General was in their midst." He later became an expert ornithologist, surrounding himself with stuffed birds and animals.

Though there are five Maynard diaries, there is very little detailed information about their lives. The diaries are tight-lipped little books filled with cryptic notations on rough weather, seasickness, camp sites, and the odd Indian adventure. Hannah kept two of them and Richard three. At their fullest they are enigmatic. For the most part, they are thin.

But there are moments: in September, 1875, they went on the mail steamer *Salvador* to San Francisco. Her journal is only a few hundred words long, but she began: "Fair wind, all sails, set, very fine. In the evening a large bird came on board, a man shot it, the wind changed." On the following day: "Still nice weather but wind right against us, mate sayes [sic] it was because they shot the bird. Maynard sick to-day, I have not been yet." (Hannah called her husband Maynard or M.) A few days later, in San Francisco, she noted with satisfaction that they had been to the playhouse, but he seems always at a distance, though they went out and bought photographic equipment and had their pictures taken together. Usually, she walked alone or with other women, and her particular pleasure on these walks was a cemetery: "Went to Lone Mountain in company with Mrs. & Miss Gerow and Mrs. Cary, it is the cemetery — got a few leaves as relics of the place, never saw such beautiful places in my life." Because of booking problems, she and Maynard returned home by steamer in separate compartments. She did not refer to him again as they travelled through huge swells in a heavy fog that she found very beautiful. She felt sorry that all the ill people around her could not see the beauty for the fog and their sickness.

These are not even notes. These are squibs and little signposts. But even so, there are touches true to their characters. She was imaginative and unafraid of theatricality, omens and the mordantly beautiful. She was to some extent literate. She was hard working and healthy as a horse, and though fascinated by death, never languid. He was hard working, and though at ease in the wilderness, entirely practical and interested in the mechanics of things. He sought no stage and seemed to flee hers from time to time. He was hardly literate and always carped about his aches and pains. In this way, they were dissimilar, but there is no evidence of discontent between them. The 1875 diary, however, concludes with a January 1876 entry — a series of quotations that constitute some sort of commentary:

> One spirit loves and loves but him,
> Like some poor girl whose heart is set
> On one whose rank exceeds her own.
>
> And dear to one as wine sacred
> to dying lips, is all he said.
>
> Oh what a tangled net we weave
> When we practice to deceive.
> *Eliott*
>
> I could not if I would transfer
> The whole I felt for him to you.
> *Tennyson*

> I never loved a tree or flower
> but 'twas the soonest to decay.
> *Arnold*
>
> He either fears his fate too much
> Or his deserts are small
> Who dares not put it to the touch
> To win or lose it all.
>
> Who changes the name
>   and not the letter
> Changes for worse
>   and not the better.
>
> Tis better to have loved and lost
> Than never loved at all.
> *Tennyson*
>
> Oh there is nothing in life half so sweet
> As love's young dream
>   (E.G.)
>   '75 (January)
> George Davidson
> G.L.H.E.M.
>
> Oh there is nothing in life half so sweet
> As love's young dream.

No George Davidson is (or it may be Davitson) ever mentioned in connection with her. The initials are also a mystery, though three children were named George, Lillian and Emma, and her own initials are H and M. Depending on how it is read, the catalogue of quotes suggests unrequited love or merely an idle exercise in conventional wisdom.

The next diary was kept by Hannah in 1879, at a time when their businesses were doing well: she in the studio, he in the field and in the shoe store. Richard had just returned from Sitka, Alaska. The *St. Louis Practical Photographer* announced in its September editorial notes: "Again they come, all the way from Alaska and Victoria, B.C., the most interesting views we have ever seen from those far-off regions." They travelled together on an excursion around Vancouver Island. The diary, dated August 13-22 and written on board the *Princess Louise*, is remarkable for its flatness of tone and paucity of reflective detail from a woman of such lively, even surreal imagination:

"Aug. 13th Left Victoria on board the Princess Louise ¼ past 8 with a party of 40 ladies and gentlemen bound on an excursion around Vancouver Island. Passed Race Rocks ½ past 9 down the straits past the "Gem of the Ocean" on the rocks. Went off Barkley Sound and anchored at Alberni at 9 in the evening. A large fire close by the mill. Expect the mill will be burnt down before the morning.

"**Thursday 14** Nice morning but too foggy to take photographs. A lot of gentlemen gone ashore for a hunt. The mill is standing. Mr. Clark, an old neighbour of ours has just come on board....He says the Indians have been holding a potlatch by the mill and their fire caught the sawdust that is what caused the fires. He has men there now trying to put it out. I suppose we will leave here soon as the whistle has blown to call the huntsmen on board. We have several seals since we have been anchored here...

"**Sat. 16th** Lovely morning so we were called early to get up. We are now on top of a high rock taking a view of the indian camp whilst Maynard down to his tent, me on the top with the cameras. 3 indians came up with nothing on but a piece of old blanket, however they did not kill me. We took two negatives when the whistle blew for the starting, so it was pack up and off for the steamer...

"**Mon. 18th** A canoe with 7 of our gentlemen, 4 indians, and 2 indian guides left the ship at 4 o'clock to go overland to Ft. Rupert. They have to go about 5 hours travel in canoe, then overland [one of these gentlemen that Hannah is describing so objectively was none other than Richard, as reported in a colorful story in the *Daily Standard*: one of her fellow travelers, when asked if a horse could have made the trip, replied he did not know but certainly seven asses had succeeded]. The steamer left at the same time. Heavy swells. Rounded Cape Scott at 9 o'clock. Anchored at Ft. Rupert at one. Had dinner then went ashore. Visited the Fort. Saw Mr. and Mrs. Hall. Went through the garden belongs to the Hudson Bay Co. Mr. Hunt is manager. Had all the black and red currants, raspberries and strawberries we could eat. Nearly all the Indians gone off to a potlatch. Could get nothing to buy. The overland party got in about dark. Very tired and wet as it came on to rain about 5 o'clock...

"**Tues. 19th** Left Ft. Rupert at daylight. Still raining smooth weather all the time now. Too foggy to land at Alert Bay. Got to the head of Frederick at 15 to 2. Turned round and went back again. Mountains thousands of feet high. Still raining. Went through Arran Rapids. Skookum Chuck at 20 min. to 3 o'clock. It takes a pretty good steamer to go through. We are now on our way up Bute Inlet. The scenery very grand but we cannot enjoy it as it is so wet. Arrived at the head of Bute Inlet, into Waddington Harbour at ½ past

6. Some have gone ashore. No indians here. Nothing but high mtns. on both sides. Some of them 8000 feet high..."

It was at this time that Hannah's eccentricity and genius began to emerge, for she began to create her Gems of British Columbia — hundreds and then thousands of children's little faces interlocked in greeting cards, putting them into photographs of potted plants and abalone shells, in frames and diamond shapes, wreaths, palettes and crosses. She also began to take portraits of herself that were full of sardonic humor as she played several parts at once on one plate: peering at herself, unmocking, perplexed, stern-faced, puzzled and preposterous, and usually in a black dress. These portraits, of course, for all their aesthetic attraction and experimentation, were always an extension of her studio work, her livelihood, and years later, after fifty years in business, she could easily brag that she had taken the portrait of everyone in town. Men and women, now elderly citizens, remember sitting in her house as little children: "There was Mama, keeping a firm grip on Simon's shoulder so he would not move, and trying not to smile at Father's stern expression. The reason Father was holding his head so high was because that starched high collar scratched his chin. And just look at Samantha, practically weeping because she had to stand on that poor dead polar bear! Just a few more minutes...everyone still. There! Mrs. Maynard was almost hidden by black cloth, working behind the huge black box, the camera..."

During these years, when Hannah was experimenting and pushing new techniques to their limit, Richard seems to have sought his own space in the wild interior or along the north coast among Indians and ice floes. He was hired as official photographer by several government agencies, commissioned, for example, to travel around Vancouver Island with the Superintendent of Indian Affairs in 1873 and 1874; and then, several times between 1881 and the turn of the century, to photograph construction along the Canadian Pacific Railroad. He went to Alaska three times, in 1879, 1882, and 1887, and to the Queen Charlotte Islands in 1884. Curiously enough, as soon as he returned, Hannah went alone to the same islands on her own expedition. Finally, he was hired to provide photographs for an international commission investigating sealing rights and seal hunting, and to do so, he went to the Pribyloff Islands in the Bering Sea in 1892.

It is an aspect of his work that nearly all his photographs, even of villages, are empty of people. It seems he sought a release from his wife's world of cascading baby faces, and her own face repeated over and over, and rooms hung with pictures of their dead. His diaries are even more uneventful than hers, made up of plaintive bleats about the weather, his health, the names of boats, how long he was on shore, and camera shot inventories. They are empty little books, but then, during the last trip to the sealing grounds, he kept a journal that is touching, if it is read as a whole.

The diary, for the month of July, 1892, was kept in a small memoranda book that had been sent out as advertising from San Francisco by the Dr. Liebig & Co. International Surgical Institute and World Dispensary. He filled the ruled blank pages on the right with his usual squibs and half-notes: "Foggy all the morning went on shore about noon with the Captain took a view looking out the Harbour with Two Whalors coming in then we went over to Dutch Harbour and I took that again because the weather was better...fine weather can just see the outline of 2, U, g, ½ past 5 evening just rounding Rose Spit going out to Sea Strait for Alaska...."

Opposite these notes, however, is an advertisement on behalf of Dr. Liebig and his cures:

Words to all in Despair.
The reason thousands cannot get cured is easily explained. There are so many different causes of Seminal Weakness, Impotency, Loss of Vitality, Memory, Sight, Hearing, Feelings, Mental and Physical Debility, Imbecility, etc. Now, any of the above diseases can be brought on by different causes, and each cause needs its own peculiar remedy. Onanism — self-abuse — may cause the above diseases and symptoms which require a certain treatment; excessive sexual indulgence may cause any of the symptoms and different medicine cures. Anger, grief, anxiety, mental trouble, exposure, hard work, poor nourishment, etc., may cause any of the symptoms of Seminal Weakness, Impotency, Indisposition, Diseases of the Liver and Kidneys, Mental and Physical incapacity, yet each peculiar case requires, scientifically used and prepared, its own remedy. It is child's play to depend on one remedy to cure all the forms of disease. Temperament, color of the eyes, hair, disposition, employment, age, circumstances, etc., have to be taken into consideration. Reader, if you are a sufferer, call or write and have your disease cured by an educated college physician — one who can discriminate and treat your disease intelligently, and give you the proper remedies. Young and Middle-aged Men, whose strength is gradually wasting away, should have a consultation at The Liebig Dispensary, before all hope of restoration is gone forever. Examine the urine; if any ropy sediment or brickdust appears, remember that it is the second stage of Seminal Weakness. By long experience in the treatment of Special Diseases of Men, we can guarantee rapid and permanent cure in curable cases. No miracles performed. We claim no supernatural power.

Spermatorrhoea — Dr. Liebig's Invigorator No. 1
Animating, strengthening and restoring.
This wonderful remedy, extracted from the rare plants growing in Southern climates, is now acknowledged by chemists as the greatest tonic and curative agent for restoring the sexual and Genito-Urinary organs to a normal condition. Sufferers from Seminal Weakness, Impotency, or Diseases of the Kidneys and Bladder, send for Dr. Liebig's Invigorator No. I, it is guaranteed to be the most powerful remedy known.

Trifle no longer, the day will come when your case will be beyond reach of the greatest remedy known to medical men. When the involuntary seminal emissions, connected with self-abuse or sexual excesses, have continued for some time, there is produced a state of enervating, a weakening of the Life force, characterized as "Spermatorrhoea."

[Interrupted by a scribbled note: "Very sick crossing the Sound".]

Prostatorrhoea — Dr. Liebig's Invigorator No. 2
Prostatorrhoea, 'Not Spermatorrhoea — treating the wrong disease.'
Many a poor sufferer from Chronic Prostatis or Prostatorrhoea has gone to a premature grave for want of proper treatment. Thousands are taking medicine to cure Seminal Weakness, Spermatorrhoea and Impotency, and yet are not troubled with the disease they are being doctored for. The real disease is usually Chronic Prostatorrhoea, and not one in ten takes the proper medicine.
Chronic Prostatorrhoea is a long-continued inflammation of the prostate. Thoroughly educated physicians alone can treat this disease successfully. The many failures to cure so-called Seminal Weakness, Impotency, Nervous Debility and Lost Vitality is due to the fact that the disease, in nine cases out of ten, is Chronic Prostatorrhoea, and the remedy taken intended to cure another disease called Seminal Weakness, or Spermatorrhoea. The symptoms in the several diseases and Prostatorrhoea are very similar, yet the treatment is entirely different. The causes of the two diseases are, in some particulars, the same. The complication of Seminal Weakness and Prostatorrhoea was discovered at "The Liebig Dispensary," and already many who could not get relief have been rescued and restored to health and strength. And a second complication has lately been discovered that prevents the cure of both Spermatorrhoea and Prostatorrhoea. The name of the second complication is known only to the Examining Physician of "The Liebig Dispensary," and will not be made public, but will be explained to the persons under treatment.

I am not sure how this is to be interpreted. Perhaps it should not be interpreted at all. Perhaps it should stand only as enigmatic counterpoint.

Whatever one makes of Richard, Hannah was energetically alive in the life around her, fascinated by people's faces, their presence. She surrounded herself with photographs of hundreds of strangers and nearly all her neighbors, catching most of the town folk while they were in and around the cradle. These cradle pictures were crucial to the development of her experimental work, and though her experimental photographs are few in number, they contain a mysterious and rare vision.

She had been working for nearly twenty years before her eccentricity emerged, but suddenly, she seemed to be in touch with every new photographic technique, exploring and expanding these techniques. Her Gems of British Columbia are a case in point.

The "gem," a small and sometimes tiny tintype featuring three or four faces of a loved one, had been around for a few years. Produced by cameras with four or more lenses, it was often mounted in a piece of jewelry — a ring, pin, or brooch. The popularity of these "gems" — and Mrs. Maynard must have made some in the 1880s because she was a master of miniatures — ended with the decade. In 1881, however, she turned the whole idea inside out and produced a monumental gathering of miniatures, a field of hundreds of tiny baby faces in montage.

These were children she had photographed during the year. She cut out each little head and body, rephotographing and reducing some, and pasted them all onto a background, often a sheet of glass in a window frame. She then rephotographed the whole. The Gems were intended as studio promotion and were sent to friends and parents of the children. They are fanciful and clever in their composition, and between 1884 and 1895 they were shaped by an obvious symbolism. Certainly, they touched the editors of the *St. Louis And Canadian Photographer* in the heart, for in early 1886, after receiving her Gems for five straight years, they not only published the 1885 version, but added the following:

"Again we present our readers with British Columbia Gems, from the art gallery of Mrs. R. Maynard, in the great North West. This is the fifth year of the gathering, and they increase in number and variety year by year. Mrs. Maynard is deserving of much praise for her skill and patience in the arrangement of these precious gems. Indeed, where can be found gems more precious. We will let the St. Louis Poet sing their praise:

Gems of British Columbia.
1881, 1882, 1883, 1884, 1885.

See this cluster of sweet faces,
Happy childhood's charming graces;
In all their beauty thus arrayed,
By Mrs. Maynard here portrayed.

Baby boys and girls are seen;
Some are smiling, some serene;
Some charming in their youthful glee,
No other gems so fair to me.

Rare and beautiful gems are these,
Wafted here by a northern breeze;
From the land of the great North West,
Where these jewels are loved the best.

These gems are gathered far and near,
Increasing numbers year by year;
The land is gleaned both far and wide,
Where e'er these precious gems doth hide.

Here are diamonds, rubies pearls,
'Mong this group of boys and girls.
Eyes that shine like diamonds bright,
Sparkling in their golden light;

Pearly teeth as white as snow,
And cheeks that like the ruby glow;
All artistically arrayed,
Brightest gems are here displayed.

Here are jewels of eighty-one,
Sparkling brightly in the sun,
Also jewels of eighty-two,
Pure and bright as morning dew.

Magnify and you will see,
Lovely gems of eighty-three,
More gems we add in eighty-four,
From that far off distant shore.

The center group is eighty-five;
Long may this artist's name survive,
And adding still more gems to these,
To send broad cast far o'er the seas.

And now our casket is complete.
With these precious gems so sweet,
With all their pretty hair and eyes,
Clear and bright as summer skies;

With all its charms both grave and gay,
We now will send it on its way,
Adown the sunny path of fame,
To bless the artist Maynard's name."

Upon close examination, however, the Gems are not so obvious and shallow as the poem suggests. There is more to them than a technical mastery predicated upon patience. They are fascinating and mysterious, and the mystery starts with the confusion over when she actually started making Gems.

It has been assumed that the first Gem was composed in 1880 because the delicate work — "Sprays From The Gem Fountain" — has that date written on the plate. It shows some sixty babies afloat on little clouds in an abyss of black. They are spray from an elaborate fountain of stacked lilies, flowers that form the base for several ghost-like Pans trumpeting children into the air or feeding cornucopias of water back into a reflecting pool. It is a little elaborate and sophisticated for a first experiment, especially as the Gems for the following three years are wooden and unadventurous by comparison.

In fact, if one looks carefully, Gem 1880 contains in the flow from the fountain several miniatures — little eighth-of-an-inch squares filled with hundreds of pin-point faces. They are the

Gems from 1881 to 1884 that so captivated the editors of the *St. Louis And Canadian Photographer*. This confusion has been caused by someone painting 1880 onto the plate, but the confusion is useful because it leads us to look closely at other Gems. They contain several surprises.

The first three montages are hundreds of faces laid out cheek-by-jowl, and they share an intricate busyness at the bottom. For example, in Gem 1881, there is not only a little girl filling a pitcher from a stream — who will show up again in a cluster of faces contained in an abalone shell — but there are strange ghostly boys and girls, one almost too small for the naked eye to find. In Gem 1882, there are more of these all-white creatures: three girls, one of them holding a bird, and a little baby spirit figure sitting in a bowl on a pedestal. Then, in 1884, when the Gems themselves took on a symbolic shape — in this case a painter's palette — two ghostly girls show up on either side of the sea of babies, one smiling and holding a bird, the other weeping with the dead bird in her hand. In next year's Gem, a series of interlocking diamonds, there are four spirit figures: a boy carrying a shovel, a boy with his shovel at rest, and two girls — one holding a bird in a cage, the other looking back into the distance, the cage empty. Such figures occur from time to time until Gem 1895.

The little white figures raise interesting questions: why are they there, and how did she make them a pure white while retaining features and expressions? Well, if one looks at the events of her life they represent a deep and abiding grief, for the series of deaths that overtook her after December, 1883, the year Lillie, her beautiful daughter, died. These figures may have begun as technical tricks, but the gravedigger and the weeping girls with dead birds end as a symbolic and poignant statement. Mrs. Maynard made no secret of her grief and informed the *St. Louis And Canadian Photographer* of Lillie's death. They responded again:

"We received some days since a letter from our friends, Mr. and Mrs. Maynard, of Victoria, British Columbia, announcing the death of their youngest daughter, 16 years of age. We deeply sympathize with them in their bereavement. Yet what is their loss is her gain. She is spoken of by those who knew her as being a very lovely character, whom to know was to love. 'Tis hard to lose our children at any age; still more so where they grow up and become more our companions than our children. She has left this world of pain and care, and entered a home reserved for the good, the bright, and blest. And when life's pilgrimage is ended she will meet them at the River where the surges cease to roll.

> *Across Death's dark and cold, cold river.*
> *Another loved one journeys on.*
> *Without a fear, without a quiver.*
> *Without a pain, without a groan.*
> *Her body here in churchyard buried.*
> *In Death's cold grasp, beneath the sod.*
> *Her spirit, by the angels guarded.*
> *Took heavenward flight to meet its God.*
> *Her pilgrimage on earth is ended:*
> *She's gone to meet the happy throng*
> *Of heaven's joyous countless millions.*
> *Who welcome her with gladsome song.*
> *Another link of chain is broken.*
> *A vacant chair that none can fill;*
> *The past is all that's left a token.*
> *Her memory lingers round as still.*
> *And when this earthly turmoil ceases.*
> *When freed from trouble, toil and care.*
> *May loved ones meet in fond embraces.*
> *And in her heavenly glory share."*

But grief and intent aside, we are left wondering how she created the little spirit creatures. We know such figures were popular in the late 1880s and that they were called photos-culptures. From an article that appeared in *Scientific American*, 1888, (reprinted from the French journal, *La Nature*), we have the procedure for creating their contradictory effect — a sardonic appeal to posterity made by the appearance of a spirit sculpted in stone.

The sitter, for example, could pose behind a papier maché bust severed at the throat. Once the photograph was taken and the real head had deceptively attached itself to the papier maché "stone," the unwanted parts of the image were either scraped from the dry negative or a print was made and then touched up with red or black watercolor paint. There was, however, a more complicated method, usually used by Hannah: unwanted parts of the body, like arms severed at the elbow, were covered with black cloth and the rest of the body, especially the subject's hair, eyebrows, and clothes were covered with a white powder. The result was a sculpted stone spirit, or the appearance of one, standing in a photographic gesture that suggested the shadow on the other side of the mirror. Hannah called these figures "Living Statuary" or "Statuary from Life", but far from picking up on a popular fascination in the late 1880s, she had mastered the techniques by the beginning of the decade. The evidence is there in the fascinating Gems.

Her most adventurous work, however, had to do with double images or multiples, something more magical than cut-and-paste montage or photosculpture. What she and others were after was the apparent suspension of the same person twice in the same space at a single moment — a person standing beside or opposite his double on one exposed plate. This touched an enthusiasm in the air: the suspicion that there was a Dr. Jekyll and a Mr. Hyde in all of us, a "wraith of the living" or "secret sharer," as Conrad called him, the "fetch" or "Doppelgänger." This was coupled with an interest in seances and spiritualism, the shadow that seemed frozen on a glass plate. After 1883, the year her daughter died of typhoid, Hannah met with spiritualists, among them the mayor of the city, and one of the family remembers going as a child with her to a seance. As more of her loved ones died, several specific photographs became icons of the dead, and these dead had their special place among her doubles.

The idea of a double or triple image, however, is rooted not only in a feeling for the dead and secret sharers, as well as theories of two personalities, but in mirrors and the possibilities of infinity contained within them. She experimented with mirrors even in her earliest portrait work. There were, of course, professional photographers who thought such experimenting was no more than trickery... "a popular form of freak photography ...work almost exclusively confined to amateurs." But that was a prim view. Hannah the professional not only pursued the technical problems posed by multiples, but she pushed her surreal and sometimes macabre sense of things to the limit.

There were, for example, several ways of showing that a man could play cards with himself or a man could carry his head in a wheelbarrow, or juggle his head in the air — all images of decapitation. Initially, a black background was the key, because it meant juxtapositions could be arranged in a visual limbo: time and place could be suspended in a darkness that hid the seams of reality.

If one wanted, for example, to portray a man talking to himself, each half of the plate was exposed separately, allowing the figure in black limbo to be taken twice on the one plate. The simplest way to do this was by using a lens cap, but there were several refinements, as explained in Cassell's 1911 Cyclopedia of Photography:

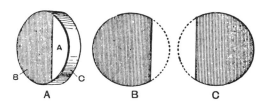

Cardboard Cap to Lens, Used in Producing Doubles

For the partial lens cap method a lens cap is made of blackened cardboard, as A, the ring C being made to fit easily the front of the lens, and then covered on one side with blackened cardboard B from which a segment is cut off as shown at A; exactly how much to be cut away should be found by trial. Having cut away a very small portion, the partial cap is placed on the lens and the picture examined on the ground glass. The cutting away must be continued until one half of the picture is dark and the other half lighted. the dividing line as seen on the screen will not be cleanly cut, but will have a diffused or vignetted effect. About the proportion shown on the right-hand side will have to be cut away, certainly not one half of the card, as might be supposed. During the cutting, the cap is revolved on the lens mount so that both halves of the view can be seen, and when one half vignettes or merges into the other a trial plate may be exposed. It requires accurate cutting to allow of one exposure merging into the other, and to prevent the join between the two separate exposures being distinguished. If, for example, a thin under-exposed band shows down the centre of the plate the covering part B is too large, and not enough has been cut away; if, on the other hand, there is a dense over-exposed strip, the aperture A is too large, thus causing the centre to receive a double exposure. To use the cap, it is placed on the front of the lens with the opening on the righthand side, as in B, and the sitter is then posed and focused on the half (left hand) of the screen on which the picture is seen, exposure shutter set, dark-slide put in, and the exposure made in the usual way, the shutter of the darkslide being drawn out all the way. For the second half, the camera must not be moved, the slide is closed, taken out, and the partial cap revolved to the opposite side — that is, to the position shown at C. The sitter then assumes a position that will be visible upon the second half of the focusing screen, the partly exposed plate is again inserted in the camera, and the second exposure made on the unexposed half of the plate. Obviously the two exposures must be of exactly the same duration. For this method the camera must be provided with a shutter working behind the lens.

If the camera has no shutter, and exposures are made by removing the cap, a cut cap cannot be used. The circular card from which the segment has been cut off, and without a ring, can be fitted into the lens hood itself, and of course covered over with the ordinary cap with which the exposures are made.

Another favourite plan of making doubles is to fix a card in the reversing back of the camera (see D), the card being blackened and a size to cover one half of the plate. The first exposure is made with the card at B, so as to photograph the half marked A; the card is then removed to A in order that the remaining half of the plate B may be exposed. The card used at the back needs to be cut even more accurately than that used in the lens, because being so near the plate the dividing line between the two exposures is more clearly cut. It is desirable to select a background with vertical lines which will not clearly show the division — a bookcase or a door, for example — and the inevitable line between the two parts of the image is so arranged that it coincides with a strongly-marked natural line in the view.

D. Card in Reversing Back

Another accessory (somewhat analogous to the first method described) is shown at E. This is a box of very thin wood, blackened inside, about 6 in. long, 3 in. deep, and 4 in. high; it has a round hole cut in the centre of the back part so that it may be fitted on the front of a lens and used as a kind of partial lens cap. The front of the box is fitted with a sliding panel or half lid, which slides across the front in grooves, allowing each half of the plate to be exposed in succession. Over all there is a proper lid which serves as a cap. This box front is used after the manner of the partial cap, and the exact width of the sliding panel can only be found by experiment as before, one side of the sliding panel being cut accordingly. The latter may be worked by a knob on the centre of the panel itself, or by means of a wire.

In all cases it is advisable to arrange the whole scene first, and to allow the sitter to try both positions, examining the ground glass carefully to see that all is included, and that no part of the sitter — feet, and legs, for example — gets beyond the centre, or the whole effect may be spoilt.

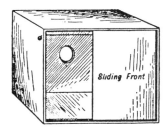

E. Box to Fit on Camera Front

There was also a technique involving mirrors, for if the "sitter" was placed in front of two mirrors inclined to each other at an angle of 90 degrees, three images would appear in the mirror; at 72 degrees, four images; at 45 degrees, seven images; and if the mirrors were parallel, theoretically the self would be reflected into infinity:

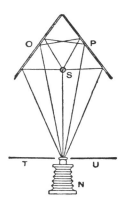

Arrangement for Multiple Photography

An exposure was made and the developed negative revealed not only a back view of the sitter, but reflected images in profile and three-quarter positions. The lines in the diagram indicate the movement of light from the subject to the mirror and back to the camera.

This was fairly elementary for a person seriously engaged in experiments in the late 1880s, and by the end of the decade, Hannah had produced quadruple and quintuple portraits of herself. In one, five figures of herself are holding a seemingly unbroken garland of flowers, but such plates were only a beginning. In 1894, the *St. Louis And Canadian Photographer* reported that it had photographs "on the freak order, showing Mrs. Maynard in different positions on the same plate." Because of internal evidence (floor patterns in a house vacated in 1892), these "freak" photographs are probably a sequence that features three portraits of herself: one, seated at a writing desk; another, staring into the camera while holding a bouquet of flowers over the desk; and another, holding a fan over her seated figure's shoulder. There is, as we shall see, a magical sense of reality to this domestic scene and an obvious romanticizing of the self.

By 1893, however, apparitions of the grotesque appeared in her multiples. Her grandson, Maynard, living with her because his mother had drowned and his father was an alcoholic, entered into her visionary world. In one photograph, he is kneeling at her knee while his double dangles a locust over her seated figure. Another double gapes at the scene, as if watching madness. It is a remarkable photograph, complex and highly suggestive, but it is only a prelude to a later scene in which he is staring in wonder at his "sculpted" body impaled on a pedestal, surrounded by photographs of Hannah's dead daughters. The fact is, by the mid-1890s she had moved into an eccentric universe all her own, achieving an aesthetic statement unmatched by photographers until the 1920s.

She apparently ceased experimenting with reality around 1897. The dated Gems conclude at 1895; photosculpture no longer interested her; and while she did a remarkable portrait of her granddaughter, Laura Lillian, as a 3-dimensional bas-relief, her playfulness and mordant sense of the deceptive eased and settled into routine.

Her sometimes bizarre vision, however, lies at the heart of all photography. Though her experimental work explored extremes, all duplication, no matter how mundane the material, implies duplicity, a lie that tells a truth. It is hard to say what truths she was after, if she was after any at all, but the vision is there, fact and fantasy frozen as one on a glass plate. She was the real thing, a parochial talent whose work is alive in the larger world because she was never provincial.

Richard Maynard died in 1907 and was succeeded by the General as the house photographer in charge. Hannah retired in 1912 and died in 1918 when she was 84. *The Colonist* reported: "Although deceased had all her life enjoyed the best of health, never having been a day confined to bed through sickness, advancing years had left their mark and the end was not unexpected...." At the funeral, the hymn *Just As I Am* was sung as the pallbearers, all grandsons, carried the casket. She was put down in the family plot at Ross Bay Cemetery.

A portrait of Richard and four of their five children: Zela, George, Emma and Albert. Early 1860s.

Richard, in a portrait from the early 1890s, is peering studiously into an English field camera. He is in front of a backdrop that daughter Lillie probably painted. It will appear in more detail in a portrait of a penny-farthing bicycle. Richard, respected in the community, was sometimes described by bemused officials he worked for as a "plucky man" who did very good work, "considering that the 'artist' is an old shoemaker lately transformed into a photographer."

This portrait is as close to calendar art as Hannah ever got.
In their later years the Maynards owned a farm, but they were only gentlemen farmers. Except for straw hats, the starched apron, the rakes and the armful of hay, they are dressed in their genteel best. The pastoral scene is a painting of a country home at Cadboro Bay owned by Richard's brother, James. They went there every summer. Hannah looks almost twenty years younger than her sixty-some years because she has whitened her face and hands. In many such self-portraits, she painted a curve into her waist on the glass plate, giving herself, though she was stoutish, an hour-glass figure.

These are Hannah's rooms in the house on Douglas Street.
The eye is drawn to her by the lustrous light of the window. There is an air of melancholy about her, but it is hard to say how calculated such effects were. She obviously had an unerring eye for composition and for the play of light. Her icons to her dead are in this portrait, but their presence is not forced: Lillie's face on the pillow and daughter-in-law Adelaide's in the frame above the sofa. The photograph is from the early 1890s.

H er approach to the still-life reveals her ability
to see and value the shape of a thing in itself. Whether she photographed a cast-iron stove or a
section of railroad track, her eye was always on the object and not on the allegorical possibilities.
In this scene, she was decades ahead of the style of her time.

These lilies in a vase sit suspended in black.
Lilies were her favorite flower, both for the living and the dead. She used lilies as the base of an elaborate fountain of youth and Lillie was her dead daugher. Her own face is on the vase.

There was a dieffenbachia plant in the Maynards' parlor.
In 1884, she covered the leaves with little faces and put faces in the potting earth, too. They are faces from her early Gems: 1881 in the upper right leaf; 1882 in the bottom left leaf; and 1883 in the earth. The landscape on the jardinière is a photograph of a local landmark, the Gorge.

Hannah took thousands of portraits of children
that are remarkable for their naturalness. She always let a child find a relaxed and expressive
pose. Though her interest in children is obvious, and she was also fascinated by death, there is no
evidence that she ever took a kind of photograph that was fashionable in England at the time:
children lying dead in their coffins.

This montage of children's faces is in an abalone shell surrounded by roots in such a way that it seems suspended, as if it were a sectioned hive of children. The montage is a segment from the lower right-hand side of Gem 1881.

Another montage from the abalone shell period.
There are sisters in Gem 1881 wearing matching white dresses with tartan waistbands. The little boy, whose foot is on the head of one of these sisters, is an early photosculpture.

A fountain of youth that is the centrepiece of a Gem
marked 1880. Quite clearly, however, it contains a selection of Gems from the years 1881 to
1888, and a preliminary version appeared in 1889. A little boy is pouring these Gems into a
narcissistic pool. The body of the fountain is built from lilies. Her dead daughter was Lillie and
her granddaughter was Laura Lillie. The little boys are photosculptures.

The expansion of the Gem fountain, featuring
babies afloat on hand-painted clouds in an abyss of black, is believed to be the first Gem because
1880 has been painted onto the plate. It was probably made in 1890. All the letters of SPRAYS
FROM THE GEM FOUNTAIN are made up of faces, and the wreath below the water-mirror
holds eight other Gems. There are perhaps five thousand faces in this photograph.

Every New Year Hannah prepared a greeting card that she sent out to mothers of all the children photographed the previous year. This is the first, Gem 1881. Eventually, each card was given its own design: diamonds, an anserated cross, a painter's palette, a Cross-Patée. This sort of montage was not unknown, but she took the technique to its limit, squeezing as many faces as she could into the design, faces that lost their individuality in the playful human crush. In Gem 1881, at the bottom, there is a photosculpture of little Baby Harry Hatherly MacDonald in an egg-shell and the girl catching water in a pitcher appears in the abalone shell. As a joke, Hannah included several doll's faces, as if they were real little girls.

The design of this Gem is again a field of faces.
But there are curious gestures: the little boy in the velvet knickers is holding a flag, Gem 1881;
the boys above him have Lilliputian figures sitting on their hat brims; the fourth figure on the
bottom right is a photosculpture of a girl with a bird on her hand; and the little boy on a tricycle
has the photosculpture bust of a girl on his extended hand. There are two more tiny
photosculptures in the bottom row: a girl on a pedestal and a baby in a stone bath.

In Gem 1883, a little girl waves flags of the two previous years. It is a field of Anglo-Saxon faces, but the first little black boy appears beside the left-hand flag. To the left of the girl wearing an elaborate bonnet, a boy has Lilliputian children hung on his chest as medals. In the shadows of the left-hand corner, there is a miniature street scene: two children walking by a picket fence, a man, and a man on a horse.

Gem 1885 contains the previous years in corner diamonds.
In the Gem from the previous year, the year following Lillie's death, there was a photosculpture allegory of sorrow. This allegory is expanded upon in 1885: at the north and south points of the centre diamond, a girl holds a caged bird and then, with the bird flown, stares haplessly into the distance; and, in the middle range of the diamond, a boy with a shovel is on his way to work, and then the same boy, his work presumably done, is weeping.

Gem 1887 has a curious beetle or turtle shape.
The body and legs have been made out of small bottle-like objects, and each segment of the legs
has a letter printed on it. The forelegs read YEARLY B.C. GEMS, and the hind legs
COMPLIMENTS OF MRS. R. MAYNARD. There are two photosculpture boys mugging for the
camera on the rim of the turtle shell. The previous Gems are contained in four circles, and in the
head and tail.

For the year a second daughter, Emma, died,
the Gem is a crown. The previous year's turtle shell is a jewel in the crown, and the crossed flags
are previous Gems. There is a stuffed goat to the left of the jewel, probably borrowed from her
son Albert's collection. An eerie and beautiful photosculpture sits in the very centre of the
crown. An irony of these Gems is that, given the infant mortality rate, dozens of children from
previous years must have already been in the grave.

In 1891, Hannah Maynard returned to a broad field of faces
and built an inner frame out of other years. In the upper corridors between Gems, lone children
stand like sentinels. The letters along the bottom are constructed from children's faces.
Considering the repetitions within repetitions, and working out the permutations, there are about
22,000 faces in this montage.

This beautiful Gem, made in 1892, is tinged with sadness. Her daughter-in-law had died, and so the celebration of babies' faces is a wreath. The potted plant from 1883 is in the bottom corners, with young Chinese sentinels in the shadows. The leaves are repeated all through the wreath, but in the pot she has made a change: there are ghostly photosculptures in each. But the heads of the sunflowers are also children's faces.

Gem 1894, a cross-patée, contains a whimsical gesture: she has reversed the stem of the 9 in the date. The letters are garlands of flowers. The field of faces is looser in composition and contains few quirks. A child in the bottom row appears to be holding an Indian lacrosse stick. With the exception of the central star from 1893, the other years are not repeated and her interest in the Gem is flagging. In 1895 or 1896 she abandoned the exercise.

These photosculpture figures obviously illustrate
an allegory of loss, perhaps the departed soul. They were done in 1884, or earlier, as they appear
in the Gem of that year.

The bust of this young girl appeared on the
extended hand of the tricycle boy in Gem 1882. The figures illustrate perfectly the technique of
imposing a powdered figure from one exposure upon a pedestal from another.

This allegorical presentation of a smiling
and then weeping girl appeared in Gem 1884, the year after Lillie's death.

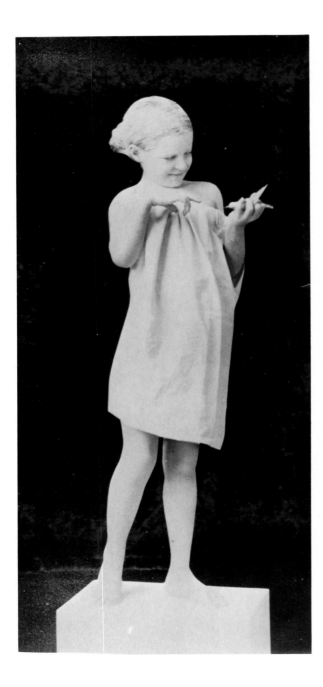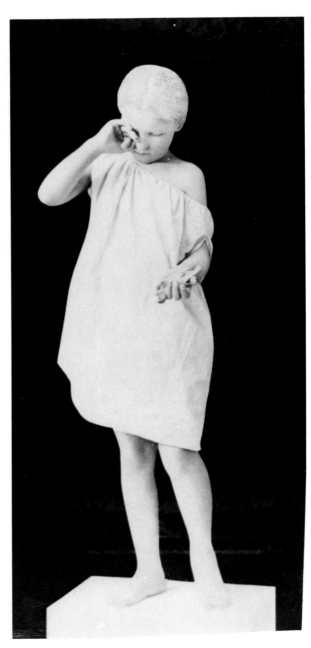

The strangest and perhaps the earliest photosculpture is of Baby Harry Hatherly MacDonald, her grandson. Born in 1880, he later became a Victoria policeman. It is likely that he played some part in Hannah's becoming official photographer for the city police in 1897. This photosculpture is reproduced in miniature in Gem 1881.

These two studies are from an early period,
shortly after her 1862 arrival in Victoria. Even at this stage, she is experimenting with the use of
mirrors for a multiple perspective.

The natural composition of the two studies is superb,
especially in its use of the backdrop as a negative space, a space devoid of domestic clutter. The
girl is her daughter, Lillie.

These little girls appear in Gem 1881.
Hannah placed a narcissistic mirror at their feet. They are studio portraits cut out and pasted to a print of previously taken photographs of rocks.

She created the mirror effect by photographing
the girl and then making two prints. One, trimmed around the feet and legs, was fitted into the
stones upside down. The two were then rephotographed together.

This is an interesting photograph because of the gawking naturalness of the reclining child and the alert pertness of the little girl. Most photographers employed some kind of mechanical device to keep children upright and rigid. The dark shadow on the right is the mother's arm. Both the boy and girl appear in Gem 1891.

There is some confusion about this portrait.
The children are Maynards and it may be an early work. The two girls look very much like
Emma and Zela as they appear in a photograph taken in the 1860s. On the other hand, they may
be grandchildren bearing the family look, as they are in Gem 1886.

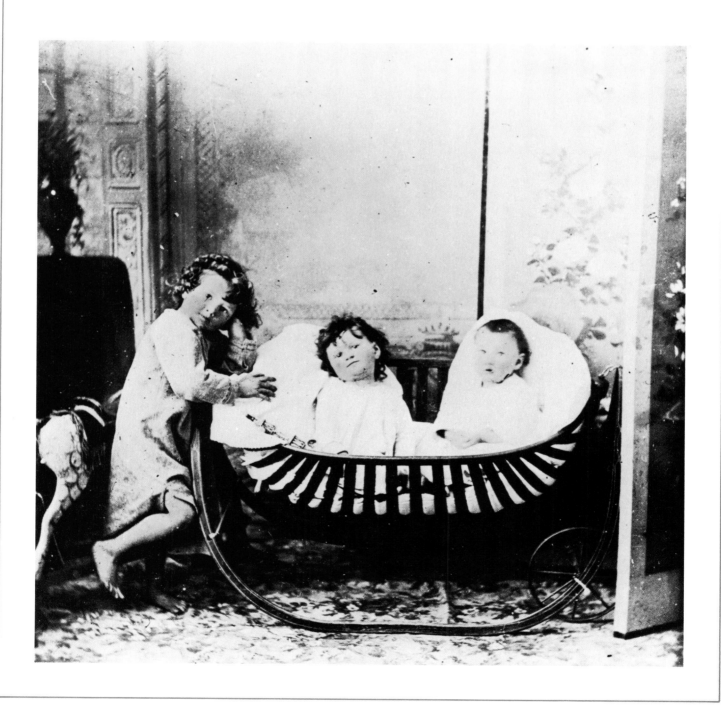

A wolverine is one of the most ferocious animals in the northwest. Though it is small, even black bears fear it. Albert, Hannah's son, was an expert taxidermist and this stuffed specimen might be from his collection, but it is nonetheless a strange juxtaposition: a pretty, pouting child sitting by a mirror pool with his hand on a one-eyed wolverine as if it were a household pet.

The two little children in palettes are found in Gem 1883, also shaped as a painter's palette. The moon-faced little boy pushing his wheelbarrow is in the diamond Gem of 1885.

A small gorge along the Nanaimo River, an area north of Victoria that opened up in the late 1840s with the discovery of coal. The Hudson's Bay Company brought English miners around Cape Horn and by 1860, large cargoes of coal were shipping steadily to San Francisco. All the surrounding landscape was extremely beautiful, dense in foliage, rivers and gorges.

Spuzzum Creek was a small salmon stream along
the Cariboo Road. The "silken" water is because of slow shutter speed, causing anything moving
to blur.

A fall of water
at Illecillewaet on the C.P.R. line.

On October 19, 1863, *The Colonist* announced that gold had been discovered in a stream beyond Langford's Lake, between the 12th and 13th mileposts on the Cowichan Trail. This was only a few miles from Victoria. Within two days, three hundred men were working on Goldstream. After six months, all dreams were disappointed. The assay reports were dismal. Then there was sudden news of a gold strike four miles away at Leech River, and the miners went there. In later years, people drove out by buggy from Victoria to picnic by the falls, shown here in midwinter. The man with the gun is unknown, but Richard placed him quite typically in the lower right-hand corner.

Millstream River is close by Goldstream.
Land Surveyors, led by J.D. Pemberton of the Hudson's Bay Company, arrived at the mouth of this river in 1852, setting up Pemberton's Encampment. Coal mines were serviced by the Esquimalt & Nanaimo railroad and shipyards built at the river's mouth. In a few years, there was a salt spring, tannery, brewery, and soda water plant. But eventually this activity petered out and the area became residential and recreational. In the photograph, the camera was set up at Belston Creek outlet on Millstream River.

Harrison Hot Springs was called Lake Qualts by the Indians, meaning "hot water." The springs, not far from the Fraser River, were found by freezing miners in 1858. Later, a circuit court judge, Matthew Baillie Begbie, wrote to the Governor: "There are some very curious hot wells...The water is hotter than the hand can bear...We gave it the name of St. Agnes' Well...a short portage...a point above the mouth of Harrison River into the lake near the hot spring which we did not visit, but named St. Alice's Well." Begbie, currying favor, chose the names of the Governor's daughters, Agnes and Alice. In 1885-6, the St. Alice Hotel was built, and by 1890 it was a favorite resort. *The Colonist* reported: "At the present time the hotel is as comfortable as anyone could desire — the table is excellent, the cuisine being under the superintendence of an experienced chef, while the vegetables are grown in a plot near the hotel and are always fresh and good. Several cows are kept so that cream and milk are always fresh and sweet, and enterprising barnyard fowls contribute their quota to the good supply. The above being the case and trout and game procurable as needed, it can well be understood that the fare served to the guests at the St. Alice is always of a tempting and palatable nature, a most desirable feature whether the guest is there simply for the pleasure, or for the purpose of benefiting his health." In 1920, the old and ramshackle hotel burned down.

In 1889, Richard went through the Bow River and Table Mountain area of the North West Territories, now called Alberta. These were not easy trips for him. He wrote in his diary: "did not get there untill 9 a clock at night & I was near death & did not intent to try to take a view but when I seen the rest all going off I had to go too, so a man offerd to carry my thing for me well we got at the Shore & it was ½ past 9 when I took the Picture...but I did not know what I was doin half the time, & it was Blowing Very strong & very cold in coming Back I had to lay down on the Beach I was so weak as I had eat nothing since I left Victoria but a little soup & than was in great Pain until I through it up again."

His 1887 diary has the following entries:
"42. From Bow River with reflection; 43. A view on Bow River, N.W.T.; 44. Pinekel Peak on Bow River; 45. Mountain Back of Fire Mountain Tributary of Bow River N.W.T. 46. Pinecal Peak from Lake..." It was sickness, weather and exhaustion that wearied and wore him down on these trips, but every now and then Indians were a danger. A friend, an historian named Gosnell, wrote: "On one occasion while photographing an Indian village, a native inhabitant, frenzied by firewater, knocked him down with a club, broke his camera and would undoubtedly have killed him on the spot had not a constable opportunely reached him."

Richard's three trips to Alaska were in 1879, 1882, and 1887. After the first trip, the *St. Louis Practical Photographer* reported in their *Editorial Chit Chat*, September 1879: "Again they come, all the way from Alaska and Victoria, the most interesting views we have ever seen from those far-off regions...Among the views before us are: Russian Church, Sitka, Mount Popoff in distance; Sitka from Alaska Island; Silver Bay, Sitka; etc." In the photograph below, taken from a steamer, the onion domes of the Sitka church are to the right; at the far left in the distance are two octagonal log bastions with cannon portals; the steamer in the foreground was called the *Julia*, and the boat-house and storage shed were owned by Linde & Hough. In the opposite photograph of a Sitka street, the church window above the scaffolding is under repair; the sign over the door on the far left says: YING KEE LAUNDRY; and the second house on the right is a bakery. The opposite bottom photograph is of Wrangell, Alaska. In his diary of 1887, he wrote: "We get to Wrangle about 1 or 2 oclock & the weather is nice now arrived at Wrangle ½ past 2 got an Indian & started for views got in his canoe & went from Point to Point took 6 5x8 & 5 8x10 then the Steamer Blew her Whistle." There are seldom any people in his photographs of villages, and there is only one person visible here.

This Indian village was photographed in 1882 or 1887. The village may be Nakusp on Arrow Lake; he described such a place in the mountains near Yale in his journal of 1887. In any case, the railroad and telegraph ran along the base of the mountain on the left, and there is a black hole into the mountain side to the right of the church steeple. It is a railway tunnel. The buildings in the village are the usual board-and-batten construction and there is not one person evident in the area.

H annah is wrapped in blankets
and wearing what looks like a deerstalker hat. This is 1889, when Hannah and Richard travelled
along the C.P.R. to Banff, Alberta. They paused for this photograph at the end of stratiform
Tunnel Mountain, near Banff. Once again, her placement in the lower right-hand corner is
characteristic of Richard.

After Richard's trip to Alaska in 1887, the *St. Louis & Canadian Photographer* reported: "An assortment of charming views of Alaska, as clean, clear, brilliant views as we have ever received from any source. 'Muir Glacier', Alaska is grand: the light and shadow is most beautifully rendered. It was taken at 9½ o'clock in the eve. There is not a bad spot in the whole 8x10 negative." There is also, escaping the notice of the editors, a lone figure in black, a man standing out among the ice floes in front of the glacier. Richard said it was "Length 70 miles — 2 miles wide — 100 feet deep." The editors then congratulated Hannah because, presumably, she had posted the pictures, and announced: "Photographers would not lose anything were they to send to this lady artist and secure a set of these views, and frame and hang them in their reception rooms. They will prove immensely entertaining to patrons while waiting."

Taku Inlet, August 18, 1882: there is no explanation for this particular photograph in Richard's diary. A steamer, probably the *Dakota,* the boat on which he was sailing, seems to have been blanketed by snow and sleet hanging like a frozen froth on the mast's crossbar and the prow. His diary of the day continues: "get 5 miles then dense fog forced us to ⊥ [his symbol for anchor] for night...Too many people got on the ice with me. It started to rock — so slippery I could hardly stand — so people in boat had to take me off." This incident was later reported in *The Colonist* of August 27, and the ice is described as breaking up with Richard in danger of drifting away, but he was rescued "from a very unenviable predicament."

At Glacier Bay in 1882, Richard captured an eerie stillness on the misty water. It is his most poetic photograph, with black figures adrift in an ice landscape, the single oar probing the white reflection in the water. His journal for August 18 reads: "Unlucky day, raining all the time. Left Harrisburg for Taku Inlet. Sailing through ice floes for 15 miles arrived as near as we could with the Steamer & then left in boats for the glacier — but could not get near for ice. So I landed on a floe to Photo. — Took Glacier & one of the floes with 2 small boats near them..."

A burned out incline along the Fraser River. Almost lost in the mist at the top of the hill, the C.P.R. line hooks around the mountain side. A single telegraph pole stands inside the rails. A fire has ravaged the hillside, leaving blackened stumps and trunks of trees. Either Hannah or Richard believed this desolation was as fascinating as pastoral scenes and exotic war canoes, the enthusiasms of other photographers. If the picture was taken by Hannah, it was on the 1885 trip; if taken by Richard in the field alone, it was in 1887, when he travelled down the Fraser Valley.

An incline of rocks and stones near C.P.R. tracks. The telegraph pole is at the top of the slope and though this seems to be a rock slide, it is probably the result of grading during construction. Either Hannah or Richard has treated the slope as if it were an aesthetic object in itself, the falling angle of ridge in tension with the upward moving piece of track. It is impossible to know what their exact aesthetic intentions were, but given the conventions of the time, the organization of both these pictures is extraordinary.

Gold mining, Douglas Island, Alaska.
In this remarkable picture, Richard has cropped not only a photograph, but the experience of the men, cutting them off entirely from any surrounding landscape. It is, for want of a better word, an existential moment seized by temperament rather than philosophical intent. The men are isolated as they cling to the rock face, and as there is no implied direction, their ladder is pathetic. Richard was on Douglas Island in July of 1887.

I n 1868, Richard and his eleven-year-old son,
Albert the General, went by steamer and wagon to the gold mining town of Barkerville. It was
the terminus of the Cariboo Road, a brawling town of little more than one straggly street, a place
of a few frame houses, some churches, sporting houses and saloons, "but home to ten thousand
souls." It was founded in the summer of 1862 when Billy Barker discovered gold in Williams
Creek. Gold was $190 a pound, and from a stake of 600 feet, Barker made $600,000, a thousand
dollars per foot. In September of 1868, shortly after Richard and Albert left the town — he with
boxes of glass plates and the boy with a nugget he'd picked up in the street — a spark from a
stovepipe set the town afire. In one hour and twenty minutes, it was gone. Richard and Albert
turned back and took this photograph of the only house left and a burned out hillside.

Taken by Richard in 1890,
this photograph won first prize in a competition sponsored by *West Shore*, a magazine in Portland, Oregon. Entitled "The Arm," it was taken from the Gorge Bridge, showing, in the words of the paper, "that most beautiful stretch of water winding inland from the harbor of Victoria, upon which the people of that city take a great deal of pleasant recreation." In the photograph, a Mr. Fred Adams is in an Indian dugout canoe with outriggers rowing to his home on the Gorge Road, and the Craigflower School is in the distance. It maybe true that in the first twenty years of her work, Hannah was professionally undercut by having to use Richard's name, but by the 1890s the tables had certainly turned. She had been congratulated for his Alaska pictures of 1887 and now the *St. Louis And Canadian Photographer* wrote: "Mrs. R. Maynard, of Victoria, B.C. has been awarded first prize in a photographic contest instituted by the *West Shore* Publishing Co. Her handsome large photograph of "The Arm" as reproduced occupies two pages of the paper. Mrs. Maynard is a popular artist in the Northwest."

There is no information about this beautiful photograph,
but it seems of a piece with others attached to the Goldstream-Millstream area. There is, in *The Colonist* of December, 1922, this remembrance of the valley as it was in the 1880s and 1890s: it "is a bewildering and enchanted ground. Boasting nothing rugged, but maintaining the soft characteristics of southern Vancouver Island scenery, its winding road...the purling of a half slumbering stream, the gorgeous colours of bordering shrubbery and trees...the unpretentious bridge, and its final long, straight arched avenue through clean-limbed trees..." This may well be a study of that avenue.

This is the purling Goldstream River,
and above it, the unpretentious bridge. Lillian, Hannah and an unidentified man are on the
bridge. At this time, in the 1880s, men still hunted panthers, cougars and deer in the valley and
often there were conflicts in the bush between Haida and Tshimpsean tribes. The Haidas often
made raids into the Tshimpsean area and took prisoners whom they hired out as slaves to white
farmers opening up territories north of Victoria.

To the left, a trestle under construction
on an Esquimalt & Nanaimo Railway bridge. The island railroad company had opened in 1886.
The train travelled at 30 miles per hour and made eleven stops between Victoria and Nanaimo. It
is not known who took this photograph, and documentation of railroad construction was
undoubtedly the main concern. But again, the aesthetic eye is unerring, and the same is true for
the 1886 photograph of a C.P.R. snowshed, opposite. A snowshed was a wooden structure built
over mountainside railroad lines. They were slope-roofed and sturdy enough to withstand snow
slides. The sections of track and trestle on the following page are of the same quality.

Hannah photographed the South Sandheads lighthouse.
It stood on iron legs at the mouth of the Fraser River. She then cut away the lower sections of
the support structure, capping it at the knees, so to speak, and set the house afloat at sea. It was
a whimsical gesture that may be attached to a strange death in her family: a relative, George
Davies, was in charge of a lighthouse and he invited friends out for a social; they were swamped
in a storm, lost their lives and he pined and pined and died a year later.

Sailing ships called at several ports
on the north-west coast: Port Blakely, Tacoma, Seattle and Victoria. These tall ships, engaged in
grain and lumbering, were elegance afloat, and Richard took many broadside photographs of
them at anchor, pictures that were popular among officers and seamen. When he himself first
arrived in this harbor in 1859, on the windship *Forward,* there was an explosion on board. Two
men standing close by Richard were killed.

Steamers and schooners
at dockside in Victoria Harbour.

One might expect that Richard the seaman
would have responded with romance to the elegance of grand sailing vessels. Instead, if his work
is compared to someone like Wilhelm Hester, a non-seaman who was a master of sailing ship
studies, it is clear that he was stimulated by the structure of things, not its outward elegance but
the mechanics. The *Mirzapore* docked at Moodyville in 1887 has a certain loveliness, but its energy
comes from the angles ajar and the cross-hatching of cables and ropes.

In the stereo of the H.M.S. *Warspite* in drydock, and the drydock itself, Richard's bent is clear: an attraction to the bones and rib-work of things. He was, at his best, a curious minimalist in allegorical times.

The shipping merchant, S.S. *City of Kingston* and its crew. With the exception of the two in the lower corners and the female cook, they have their positions stitched onto their caps: captain, 2nd officer, 1st officer, pilot, chief engineer, 1st asst. engineer, 2nd asst. engineer, purser, night officer, freight officer, 2nd steward, bar-tender, chief steward, watchman and quartermaster. Hannah has made a montage of these figures and then used paint, paper and paste on the plate to set them in smoke from the ship's stack. The plate was then rephotographed.

A self-portrait, with Hannah bent over a punt in Beacon Hill park.

Hannah and Richard are in their professional milieus:
Hannah surrounded by portraits, Richard surrounded by shoes. Richard is wearing his
deerstalker hat. Some of the boxes in the foreground read: TENNIS BALLS and a poster on the back
wall proclaims NIGRO WATERPROOF. Richard's camera sits on a tripod alongside the room divider
in front of the back door. Hannah has her own business about her: the portrait cards she sent out as
promotion, including a mélange of Chinese on the left panel of the screen. Gem 1893 is on the wall by
the door drapes along with a small photosculpture. The dieffenbachia plant she used in Gem 1883 is
in the pot held overhead by the boy statue.

An apparently simple parlor scene, with Hannah sitting at her ease, actually contains a secular altar to her dead. Daughter Lillie died in 1883; another daughter, Emma, died in 1888; and a daughter-in-law, Adelaide, died in 1892. On the whatnot in the corner, the room's altarpiece, two little vases feature the faces of Hannah and her husband. There is a portrait of Lillie on the pillow. Emma is in the frame on the table to the right, and Lillie is on the plate on the floor. There are two plates beside the whatnot bearing the faces of Lillie and Emma. A silken pillow delicately stitched with Lillie's name sits at the apex. On the left, an elaborate frame contains pictures of Lillie and Emma under a photograph of the family plot in the cemetery.

The Maynard clan gathered for a birthday
or Valentine's Day party, and Hannah, as she usually did, positioned herself in profile. Zela is
between Hannah and Richard, and their granddaughter Laura Lillian is second from the right.
The young men in front look very much like Albert's sons. He is not in the picture and may well
have been operating the camera. The man with the moustache by the piano is Arthur S.
Rappertie, Hannah's assistant between 1882 and 1904.

Hannah's most magical experimental work
depicted the multiple presence of herself. She took conventional domestic settings and turned
them inside out — surrealism decades ahead of its time. These three were accomplished through
a combination of masking and lens capping against a black background. Within a few years her
multiples became rare technical feats, as one figure impinged upon the space of another. They
also revealed her personal eccentricity: a woman intent upon herself, a woman with a mocking
and even gallows sense of humor. It is clear, in the photograph below, that she touched up her
faces, painting out the lines in her forehead, between her eyebrows, from nose to mouth, from
mouth to chin, and under the chin. The same is true for the photographs on the page opposite,
where she has strung a seemingly unbroken garland of flowers between four and five portraits of
herself. Her figure is in particularly good shape, tucked at the waist to the trim of a young girl.
There is a romance of the self in these photographs from the late 1880s.

H ere Hannah has placed herself in a much more complicated domestic setting, taking certain technical risks and solving them to a surprising extent. The two outside figures below have been retouched on the exposed plate, presumably to hide the matting seams. This is evident in the baseboard on the left and in the dresses on the right. Another seam can be found in the frame on the wall, where the line of the frame is broken. All this matting, however, does not explain how she managed to suspend the bouquet over her hand and the letter, or how she managed to lay the fan across her shoulder, impinging upon the central space in both instances. These are probably the photographs she sent to the *St. Louis And Canadian Photographer* in 1894.

These two multiples, containing the same technical mystery in the central space, are much more sophisticated. There is no obvious retouching on the plate and she has complicated the technical problem with a background of domestic clutter — aiming for more mystery and therefore more reality. In the first photograph, there is a blurred matting line under the bustle of the seated figure, and in the second, a matting line is evident down the wall and in the arch. She has, however, used indirect lighting (note the reflecting screens on the right) to cast a counter shadow on the wall, drawing the eye away from the obvious seam, or at least confusing the issue.

Despite the use of indirect lighting, the matting lines are clear in this surprising and strange photograph. Maynard, the son of her daughter, Emma (who died by drowning in Seattle in 1888), came to live with Hannah and she incorporated him into her magical world. Here, with the pole somehow crossing the obvious matting line, he is dangling a dead locust on a hook over her head. She is reading unawares while he sits at her knee holding up a warning finger, smiling. To the left, she stares moodily away from the scene while he, on bended knee, gapes.

Hannah has set herself in a scene
so determinedly staid that it finally seems insane. She has a symmetrical relationship with herself.
While holding a skein of wool, she is looking behind herself as if she, too, were searching for the
seams of reality. Off to the side, standing apart and almost out of frame, she is regarding the set
as if it were not only strange, but a little drama being played out for reasons unknown to her.
She has, however, bound herself into the tea party because she is winding wool and the line of
wool cuts directly across the picture through the tea service. There is one flaw, a break in the
wool, but it is almost hidden by the white drapery on the back of the chair. The face of her
daughter, Lillie, is on the pillow on the floor.

Her approach has become extremely rich and complicated. The mystery of the situation is openly stated through the placing of the empty frame on the floor at the far right, a frame focused on the bizarre scene. The portrait hanging on the wall is her daughter Emma, the woman on the easel is Adelaide, and Lillie is framed behind Maynard on the floor. He is staring lovingly at Hannah as she tips her hat to his severed body impaled on a pedestal. He is playing with her neckscarf while she stands behind him wearing a quizzical look, as if all this, though normal, is quite mad. The quizzical look is capped off by her garb: the peculiar diamond patterns in her dress and her jaunty hat.

This formal tableau borders on the grotesque.
Looking girlish for her age (she is 60 in this photograph) and nicely nipped at the waist, she sits to the far left looking in on the scene through a proper lorgnette. Her dead sit between her selves: Lillie, Adelaide, and Emma. She is staring directly, with all the vanity of a handsome young woman, into the camera as Maynard looks up at the severed torso of himself, impaled again as a photosculpture shadow of himself on the pedestal. It is a scene open to several interpretations, all of them unsettling.

As she sits pouring tea, her morbid sense
of herself is tinged by the comic. She is looking decidedly more her age as she stares impudently
into the camera, challenging the nature of normalcy. She is playing three parts: she is quite
proper, she is cocky, and as a studio portrait, she reaches outside its framed reality to pour tea on
her own head. Her air of disdain inside the frame is delightful.

The enigmatic character of her work
seems even stranger when one remembers that photographers and painters of the time tended to
allegorize experience to the point of sentimental simplicity. This little girl, though she is with
Hannah in the studio, is quite clearly alone with her wagon. Hannah is equally alone, wearing a
riding outfit while reading a book. In the book is Gem 1884, the year after her first daughter's
death, and there is a clean link between the white pages of the album and the girl's white dress.
In the painted backdrop, an empty boat drifts in the shadow-image of Siwash Rock.

In this 1902 portrait of Fire Chief Thomas Watson
in his office on Cormorant Street, Hannah used the direct light from the windows as a focal
point, a luminous space that holds the chief, child and stove together. The reflection of this light,
however, also seems to suspend the table, rug and spittoon in light, as if the relationship were
tenuous.

There is a porcelain quality to this lovely portrait.
The scene is a painted English garden; the women are seated close to a
fringed table placed on fake grass; one woman has her umbrella up and open; there is a
pot-bellied stove in the foreground. Although the stove would have been cropped out of any
print she might have made, the disparate pieces emphasize the essential surrealism at the heart of
photography, particularly studio work where men and women of conventionality accepted
any contradictions for the sake of a picture of themselves.
Hannah's son, Albert, is standing to the left.

In a portrait meant to be cropped, we can see
the surrounding paraphernalia of the studio: a false fireplace, a back-lit window, painted panelling,
the rolled backdrop. In this setting, the amiable family grouping seems not only frozen
nostalgically on glass, but they are unconscious coconspirators
in a theatrical deception, a deception by people who probably would never dream
of deceiving anyone on other terms. 1888.

It is rare that anyone in Hannah's portraits
stares into the camera with that fixed manic glare so common to early photography.
But here is a stern clansman who looks as if he has just seen the ghost of himself. For this
portrait, the plain backdrop has been unrolled and the family is rooted in negative space. It would
be interesting to know who made these scenic decisions, who decided that
such a man should be seen in a space as free from domestic clutter as possible. 1886.

Their son, Albert the General, and his stuffed birds. He was an expert ornithologist, a taxidermist, a magician, a collector of guns and a photographer who was manager of his father's boot business for over thirty years. The photograph is from 1890.

H annah: self-portrait, 1878.

This is not a self-portrait.
In 1867 in Victoria, there was a studio run successively by Charles Gentile, Noah Shakespeare, William M. Ashman, and Shakespeare again. In this photograph, probably taken by Ashman, Hannah is holding the newly-born Lillie. She looks more drawn and older than in any portrait she took of herself in following years.

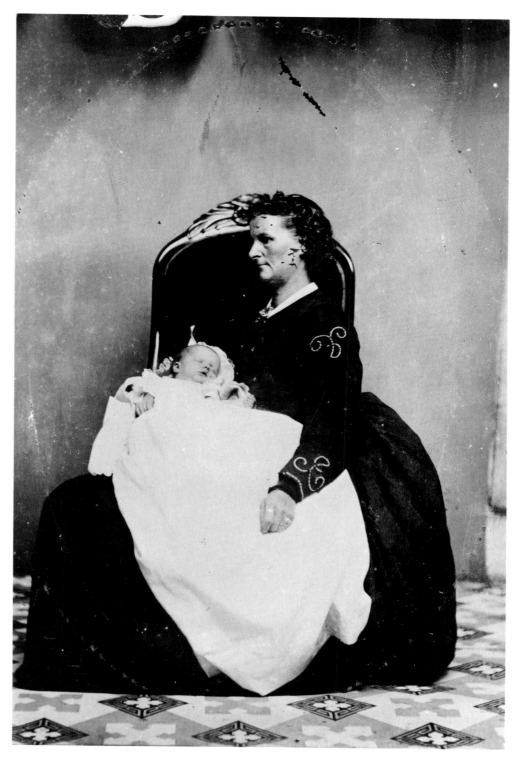

An unknown woman; late 1870s.

An unknown man and his daughters: 1885.

Clothing for boys did not vary from year to year toward the end of the century. This sleeping little fellow is in none of the Gems and so the photograph is probably from 1895-1910.

A child from Gem 1882.

A child from Gem 1882.

Children from Gem 1894.

A child from Gem 1891,
with a mother's supporting arm on the left.

An unknown woman:
because she is wearing long gloves, and because of the frill around the bouquet, she was probably
a maid-of-honor or lady-in-waiting for a wedding. Her hair style was in fashion in the early
1880s. As an indication of how individual and eccentric Hannah was, the cut of her own clothes
and the shaping of her own hair were seldom in tune with the conventional fashion of the
moment.

In 1897, Hannah became official photographer for the Victoria Police Department. She held the position for five years. Anyone arrested was marched down the street to her studio. She took the "mug shot," at first full-face, and then after a while she used a specially constructed mirror that rested on the prisoner's shoulder, providing a full-face picture plus profile on a single negative. An unsettling number of the prisoners were children arrested for theft; some were Oriental (since twenty percent of the population in the insane asylum was Chinese, it seems many anti-social Orientals ended up there); some were thugs and beguiling girls; and a few were like stylish Belle Adams, arrested for murder. The *Daily Colonist* reported in June of 1898: **'BY A WOMAN'S HAND' Charles Kincaid the Victim of His Mistress' Jealous Rage. A Johnson Street Hotel the Scene of the Awful Crime.** Nine o'clock last evening was the time of this latest tragedy of which unbridled passion and mad jealousy constitute the cause, and the scene of the horrible deed that cost Charles Kincaid his life was a first floor front room in the Empire Hotel on Johnson street. Here the woman, frenzied by the fear that her unrestrained and unnatural affection for a man not of her own race or color was no longer returned, half severed his head from his body with a razor. Kincaid — Charlie Brown as he was called in Victoria — wounded to the death, staggered down the stairs and into the street, where he fell, and within a few moments gave up his life. The woman followed him, and weeping hysterically threw herself upon the bleeding, quivering body, madly embracing it, speaking words of endearment into the deaf ears, and pleading for forgiveness and the life of the man she had struck down. Then the awful scene was ended by the opening of a way through the crowd for an officer of the law, and she was made a prisoner by Constable Anderson, to answer for the life that had been taken. The story of the affair is a plain though terrible tale..." Belle Adams obviously dressed for her final portrait, but she was only sentenced to five years for manslaughter. The convicted persons on the following pages cannot be identified by name as they are still protected by provincial personal privacy laws. The notations are from the police book.

Arrested by Sergeants Walker and Clayards, charged with assaulting his wife. This man is a scene painter, and a stranger here, and married her, as was claimed, one week after meeting, expecting money but she had none had been married only a few days when this assault took place.

Sentence 6 months in each of four counts to run concurrently April 4. Arrested by Det Perdue charged with obtaining money by false pretences, by means of "Confedssats" notes.

Reformatory Boy for reference.

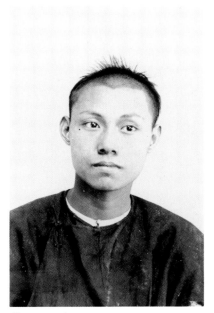

Sept. 14th, 1898 #72
Arrested by Cons. McDonald and Serg. Hawton, charged with breaking and entering three stores on Fort Street and stealing few goods to the value of $10. 3 years.

Dec. 30 1897
#27 arrested by Perdue, charged with
stealing $8.00 from an Indian.
Sentenced to 2 years.

April 2 1902
Arrested by Palmer and Perdue,
charged with stealing $220.00 from
Amos Copperwell. This woman has
previous convictions for the same
offence.

Arrested by Chief and Serg. Hawton
charged with attempted murder. This
man went into the Saloon, just as the
proprietor Noble was closing and
engaged the proprietor in a game of
cards and suddenly pulled out a gun
and demanded Noble's money. He
fired four shots, and then fled one
shot took effect. The others missed.
He was found home in bed.

Nov. 27 1900
Arrested by Det Palmer and Perdue
charged that he did kill & slay Claude
Olive Mallby.   Faith healer.

Arrested by Det Palmer and cons.
Clayards. Charged stealing from a
Dwelling house, also Breaking and
entering, by day. Possession of stolen
property.   Com for trial.

Arrested by Det Palmer, Perdue
others possession stolen property.

Arrested by Cons. Handley and
Northcott, charged with Breaking and
entering Blaquiere & Heggertys store
and stealing.

Arrested by Constable Macdonald,
charged with setting fire to the house
of Charles Marston corner of James
and Rendall Streets. (Committed for
trial) and acquitted girl was here in
95 charged with being of unsound
mind. She has since been in the
asylum.

Hannah Maynard in nine poses.

She is wearing a bicycling hat and is surrounded by a galaxy of pictures of herself. The paper is curled to read: With Mrs. Maynard's Compliments. 1887.

A n unknown woman: 1904.
The plumed hat was fashionable in 1903-4, the dress until 1910. She is in what was known as
the shepherdess pose.

A n unknown woman,
date also unknown. The technique employed was called split-lighting or line-lighting. Very few
portrait artists sought this effect during Hannah's time.

An unknown young woman,
a member of the prominent Henry P. Pellew Crease family. Many of the Crease children appeared in
Gems over the years. Sir Henry was Attorney General of British Columbia and helped lead the
Colony into Confederation in 1871: the photograph is from the late 1880s.

Hannah's granddaughter,
Laura Lillian, in 1887 when she was seventeen. She had been close to Lillie, and in a sense
replaced her cousin as the young beautiful model in Hannah's life.

In this portrait, Laura Lillian is wearing
a very fashionable silk dress with a watered moiré frill.
The curled paper effect was possible because Hannah was no longer working with a glass plate. She
was using a factory-made negative with the pattern prepared in it, or special developing paper that also
contained the rolled edges. Late 1880s.

An unknown woman: her chignon hair style
was popular in the early 1890s, and Hannah has once again split — or line-lit — the face.

This reproduction is an attempt to render
the effect of a remarkable bas-relief. Hannah, in a portrait of Laura Lillian, built up
the features of her face and body from behind, raising the shoulder puffs, without distortion,
almost an eighth of an inch. It was a complicated process in which blotting paper
was attached to the back of the print and the portrait was embossed by tooling in a circling
motion with a bone or ivory paper knife. A handbook in 1911,
long after she'd completed this portrait, advised: "The work must be done very gently,
as the blotting paper is damp, and the tool may go through and spoil it." Once the embossing
was done, it was filled with plaster-of-Paris or papier-maché. Very few successful
examples of such bas-reliefs exist in the world.

Laura Lillian was born in 1873 and she died in 1951.
She worked as a postal clerk. In this portrait, taken in 1905, she is wearing a cape-like top that was in fashion during that year.

A self-portrait set in a keyhole: late 1890s.

A very stylish portrait anticipating
the fashion photography of the following decades: 1900-1903.

Bicycling was the rage before
the turn of the century. Families in their Sunday best — and Hannah was always
very elegant — went for long afternoon rides. Young Maynard was always with her.
Richard seems to have had no interest in the event. It was, of course, still impossible to capture
men and women in motion, but Hannah, setting herself in a stationary position in this 1890
photograph, sought the illusion of movement. A small stone and an almost invisible brace were
placed by the back wheel. With her self-conscious awareness of how staged captured moments of
reality were, she photographed exactly the same scene being photographed by an unknown
young man: a duplication of her attempt
to give duplicity the air of truth.

I n these photographs she is using balancing
devices but few can be seen, even under magnifying glass. In the bottom picture, she has
positioned Maynard to the front, while Laura Lillian is moving into the distance as if they had
just passed each other on the road. There is, however, one flaw. Hannah has
moved slightly and the upper-right corner is blurred. She has drawn in the trunk
of the tree with the boughs trimmed as if the tree were dead.

This backdrop stood behind Hannah's portrait of Richard in the early 1890s. It was probably painted by Lillie. Several of her landscapes are still in the family's possession. In the late 1880s, Hannah used the backdrop as the setting for a beautiful penny-farthing bicycle. She was interested in the motion of the new social enthusiasm, but here she has concentrated on pure design, the strange symmetry that exists between the circles.

Fountain Lake, Beacon Hill Park, 1907.
A photograph taken by Hannah the year Richard died. This land had been
reserved for a public park as far back as 1858 by Governor Douglas, and the 154 acres
were always popular, not only for picnics but also for horse racing. In 1878, a two-gun battery
was installed for protection in case of Russian invasion and, eleven years later, John Blair was
commissioned to landscape the park. He created two artificial lakes, lovely flower beds, a zoo and
pleasant walks and roads for bicycles.

Cyrus H. Bowes, drugstore, Johnson Street, ca. 1900.

Queen's Market, a butcher shop
among wholesale houses, at the corner of Government and Johnson Streets, ca. 1890.

The White House, H. Young, Proprietor.
A shop for dry goods, dressmakers and millinery. 1890.

Gisburn, the residence of Robert Irving.
Corner of Belcher (now Rockland Avenue) and Moss Streets. 1890. The stone fence and gate still stand but the house, which originally cost $40,000, was destroyed in 1937.

Unknown residence. 1890s.

Mount Tolmie, the residence of George Deans, near Shelbourne Street and Hillside Avenue. He died in 1879. His wife is seated. She died in 1890, so the photograph was taken some time before that year. Their son, George Jr., is to the extreme right. George's brother James, wearing the tam, was an amateur anthropologist.

Around the turn of the century,
the family gathered for an outing at Cadboro Bay. Richard is in the centre. The least attractive of
the daughters, Zela, is to his left. She eventually married a mine owner, W. H. Smith, but in 1903
she died at sea. Her death contained its own irony, as the boat
on which she died was called the S.S. *Adelaide.* The man on Richard's right
is Rappertie, very much the dandy in the group. Hannah is half hiding
to the far left, deep in the foliage and shadow.

Zela and Rappertie are to Richard's right.
Rappertie and his sister spent many social hours in the Maynard household. There are several photographs of him in the studio and under one of them Hannah has written "Wandering Jew." He was treated as one of the family and seemed totally at ease on all occasions. Hannah is out in the open to Richard's left, presenting herself in profile.

A portrait of Richard: mid-1890s.

Rappertie is posing on a bicycle in the studio.
Hannah used an old technique to create the mirror effect. The photograph,
taken in the late 1890s, is interesting because she defined the scene by lighting her subject's
face, the front wheel, the trees and the backdrop, but she left the body and the mirror
in a field of frontal black. Her understanding of lighting was extraordinary. This is apparent
in her treatment of Richard's watch chain and black gloves
in the portrait opposite.

This is a curious photograph that cannot
with certainty be credited to Hannah although it is in
a family album of her work. It was taken on an outing to Gypsy's
Cave, outside Seattle, on July 18, 1898. At first
it seems as if it must be a mistake, caused by a flaw in the
negative or lens, but careful inspection reveals the disembodied
face hidden in the bark of the tree, the body flowing down into
the roots. There is also someone hidden in the hollow of the
giant cedar. The woman is Laura Lillian.

A picnic meeting of spiritualists at Cordova Bay, 1886. Hannah and other photographers were attracted to spiritualism, although she never tried to deceive herself or anyone else by pretending shadows and wavering presences were ghosts captured in the camera's eye. Here she is in respectable company, for the man wearing the pearly-grey top hat is the mayor of Victoria, Mr. James Fell. He was president of the spiritualists' society. Hannah, as usual, is off to the side and in profile.

Hannah and Richard at the turn of the century.
The woman carrying the parasol behind the fence is not known, but the same parasol had
appeared in several previous family portraits.

A portrait of Richard before the turn of the century.
He has been reading *The Colonist*, and though he is in his seventies, the page is folded at the travel
advertisements: famous trains to the northwest and steamer bookings for south eastern Alaska.
After he died in 1907 and his pioneering tale was told in the papers, it was pointed out that he
had been a very responsible citizen, a non-active Conservative, the treasurer of both the
Woodmen of the World and Foresters and a Companion of the International Order of Foresters,
"a man of genuine worth and wide popularity, whose life work has been valuable...all who know
him are glad to call him friend."

Hannah, a self-portrait, 1900-1905.

H annah, a self-portrait: about 1910.

H annah, a short time
before her death in 1918. Albert, in his sixties, is with her.

First Maynard Photographic Gallery,
1863-1874: corner of Johnson and Douglas Streets. 1868.

Maynard's Developing Box, ca. 1875, Victoria.

Second Maynard Photographic Gallery and Shoe Store, 1874-1892:
Corner Johnson and Douglas Streets. 1888.

Third Maynard Photographic Studio and Shoe Store:
41 Pandora Street, 1895.

Third Maynard Photographic Gallery, ca. 1900:
Pandora Street, looking East from Douglas Street.

Maynard's Float in Parade on Pandora Street, ca. 1900: Victoria.

I have received inestimable assistance in the
preparation of this book from my friends in
Victoria, Barbara McLennan, Leslie Mobbs, J.
Robert Davison and the staff at the Provincial
Archives of British Columbia.

I am particularly indebted to David Mattison for
his enthusiastic and diligent care for all details of
fact pertinent to this material.

I wish also to thank members of the Maynard
family, Mrs. Bunty Coombs, Mrs. Dorothy Reed,
Mrs. Amy Ruth Maynard, and Mrs. Grace Blake
Croft, who welcomed my interest so warmly and
provided me with insights and information of a
private, and therefore, privileged nature.

I extend my appreciation for all aid to photographs
librarian Suzan Seyl of the Oregon Historical
Society; to photohistorian Robert Johnson of
Nanaimo, British Columbia; to Mrs. Mary C.
Holford, Assistant Curator, Textiles Department of
the Royal Ontario Museum; to the Victoria City
Archives; and to Constable Gary Green and
Deputy Chief J. L. Smith of the Victoria City
Police Department.